Gladiators

by Mark Roemhildt

TORQUE™

BELLWETHER MEDIA • MINNEAPOLIS, MN

Are you ready to take it to the extreme?
Torque books thrust you into the action-packed world
of sports, vehicles, mystery, and adventure. These books
may include dirt, smoke, fire, and dangerous stunts.
Warning: read at your own risk.

Library of Congress Cataloging-in-Publication Data

Roemhildt, Mark.
  Gladiators / by Mark Roemhildt.
     p. cm. -- (Torque: History's greatest warriors)
  Includes bibliographical references and index.
  Summary: "Engaging images accompany information about gladiators. The combination of high-interest
subject matter and light text is intended for students in grades 3 through 7"--Provided by publisher.
  ISBN 978-1-60014-744-9 (hardcover : alk. paper)
  1. Gladiators--Juvenile literature. I. Title.
  GV35.R64 2012
  796.8--dc23   2011028867

This edition first published in 2012 by Bellwether Media, Inc.

Printed in the United States of America, North Mankato, MN.

Contents

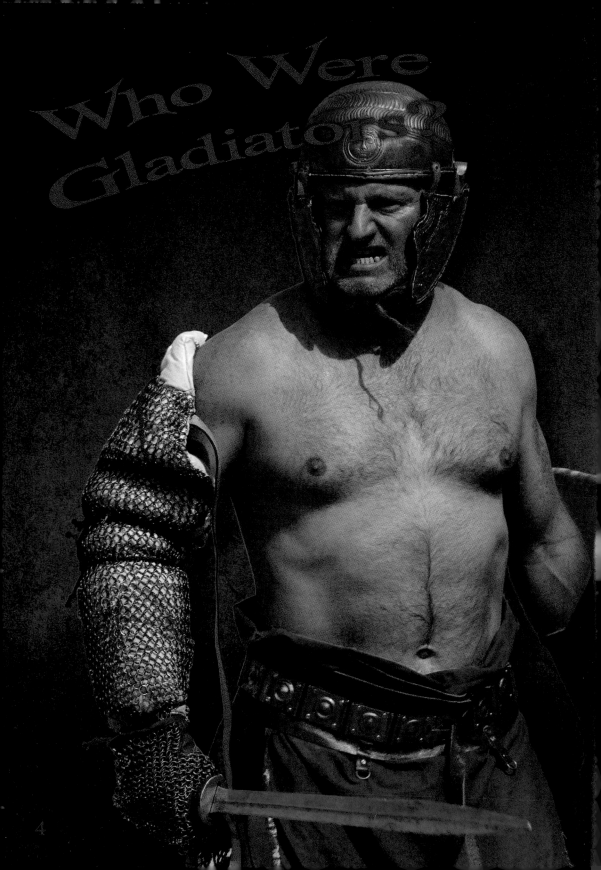

Who Were Gladiators?

Huge crowds cheered as gladiators fought during the height of the Roman **Empire**. Gladiators were not soldiers. They were entertainers. These fighters faced one another in **amphitheaters**. Gladiators gave their blood, sweat, and often their lives to perform for the people.

Gladiator Fact

The most famous amphitheater was Rome's Colosseum.

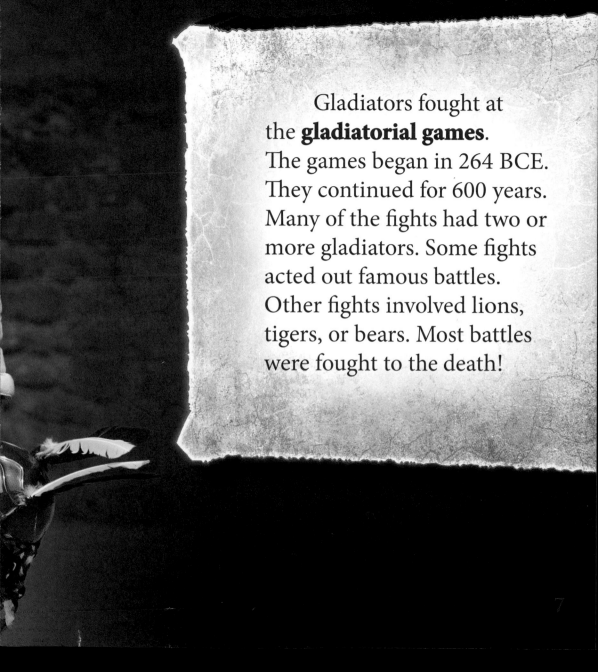

Gladiators fought at the **gladiatorial games**. The games began in 264 BCE. They continued for 600 years. Many of the fights had two or more gladiators. Some fights acted out famous battles. Other fights involved lions, tigers, or bears. Most battles were fought to the death!

Gladiator Training

8

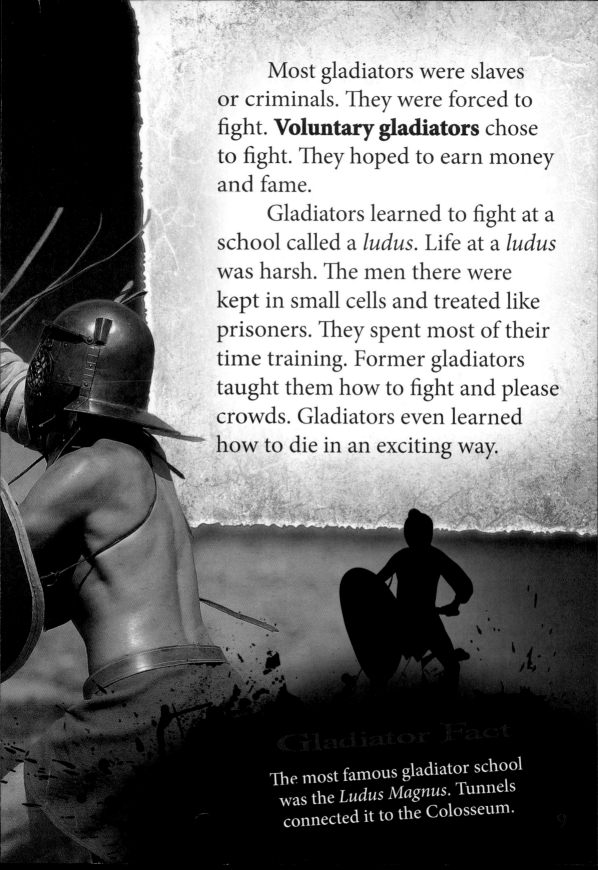

Most gladiators were slaves or criminals. They were forced to fight. **Voluntary gladiators** chose to fight. They hoped to earn money and fame.

Gladiators learned to fight at a school called a *ludus*. Life at a *ludus* was harsh. The men there were kept in small cells and treated like prisoners. They spent most of their time training. Former gladiators taught them how to fight and please crowds. Gladiators even learned how to die in an exciting way.

Gladiator Fact

The most famous gladiator school was the *Ludus Magnus*. Tunnels connected it to the Colosseum.

All gladiators took an **oath**. They agreed to give up their rights and be treated as slaves. In return, they had the chance to win money, fame, and their freedom. They could then start their own gladiator schools. These schools made money by providing fighters for the games.

Gladiator Fact

The largest gladiatorial games took place in 107 CE. The games involved 10,000 gladiators!

Gladiator Equipment

There were between 20 and 30 **classes** of gladiators. Each class used a different combination of equipment. Many fought with a simple sword called a **gladius**. Some used spears, daggers, or **tridents**. Others fought from horseback with long metal lances.

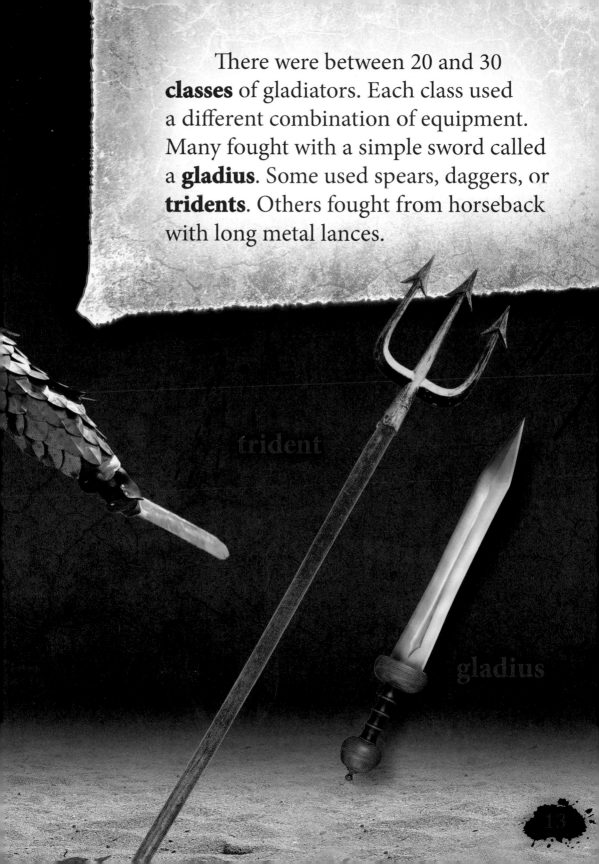

trident

gladius

The Romans wanted to see entertaining fights to the death. For this reason, gladiators were given limited armor. Some fought with nothing more than a **loincloth**. Others wore leather armor and helmets with **visors**. Some classes of gladiators were allowed leather or metal shields. The *parma* was a small round shield. The *scutum* was a large rectangular shield.

Gladiator Fact

Sometimes the crowd got to choose whether a defeated gladiator lived or died. Fans could cheer, give thumbs up or down, or wave handkerchiefs to cast their vote.

scutum

15

Gladiator Classes

Every gladiator fit into a certain class.
Each class used different equipment.

Class	Equipment
Equites	Horse, spear, gladius, arm guard, and *parma*
Samnites	Gladius, *scutum*, and plumed helmet with a visor
Thracians	Curved sword, dagger, *parma*, leg armor, and helmet
Mirmillones	Gladius, *scutum*, helmet, and arm guard
Retiarii	Trident, net, and dagger
Secutores	Gladius, *scutum*, helmet, arm guard, and leg guard
Hoplomachi	Spear, short sword or dagger, *parma*, helmet, and leg guards

Retiarius

Thracian

Samnite

17

The Decline of Gladiators

The Roman Empire began to change around 300 CE. Wars had weakened the power of the empire. More Romans were becoming Christians. Many Christians disapproved of the games. Emperor Constantine banned the practice of forcing criminals to fight in the year 325 CE.

Constantine

In 72 BCE, a gladiator named Spartacus led about 100,000 slaves in a revolt. It took the Roman Empire two years to defeat the rebels.

By the early 400s, most Romans saw the games as **barbaric**. In 404 CE, Emperor Honorius banned the games entirely. However, even that didn't completely end them. Illegal games continued for more than 100 years. Eventually this bloody form of entertainment died out. The fierce gladiators were no more.

Glossary

amphitheaters—large, curved structures with rows of seats rising around an open area; amphitheaters are stages for sporting or dramatic events.

barbaric—overly violent and uncivilized

classes—types or kinds

empire—a kingdom made up of many lands

gladiatorial games—events staged at amphitheaters that featured a series of battles between gladiators

gladius—a Roman sword; a gladiator's gladius was short, simple, and cheaply made.

loincloth—a small, one-piece cloth worn over the hips

oath—a promise to do something or behave in a particular way

tridents—spears with three prongs at the end

visors—moveable parts on the front of helmets that protected the faces of gladiators

voluntary gladiators—free citizens who chose to become gladiators in pursuit of money and fame

To Learn More

AT THE LIBRARY

Guillain, Charlotte. *Gladiators and Roman Soldiers.* Chicago, Ill.: Raintree, 2010.

Martin, Michael. *Gladiators.* Mankato, Minn.: Capstone Press, 2007.

Matthews, Rupert. *100 Things You Should Know About Gladiators.* Broomall, Pa.: Mason Crest Publishers, 2011.

ON THE WEB

Learning more about gladiators is as easy as 1, 2, 3.

1. Go to www.factsurfer.com.

2. Enter "gladiators" into the search box.

3. Click the "Surf" button and you will see a list of related Web sites.

With factsurfer.com, finding more information is just a click away.

Index